ANNECY TRAVEI
2024/2025

Exploring France: Discover the Enchanting Canals, Alpine Beauty, and Timeless Charm of the Venice of the Alps - Your Ultimate Companion for Exploring Medieval Streets, Scenic Lakes, and Hidden Gems in This Idyllic French Gem

MAXWELL CLARKE

Copyright © 2024 by Maxwell Clarke

No part of this publication may be reproduced, stored in a retrieval system, or transmitted in any form or by any means - electronic, mechanical, photocopying, recording, or otherwise - without the prior written permission of the publisher. Unauthorized use or distribution of any part of this work is strictly prohibited

Annecy Lake

Annecy Scenic View

Welcome to Annecy, France.

Table of Contents

Chapter 1 1

Introduction 1

    Geography and overview of Annecy 3

    A brief history of Annecy 9

    Why Annecy should be your next adventure destination 13

    Top Destinations and Attractions in Annecy 19

Chapter 2 35

Planning Your Trip 35

    When to Visit 35

    Getting There 36

    Arrange Transportation (Getting around) 43

    Prepare for Activities 44

    Pack Appropriately 47

    Final Preparations 54

Chapter 3 61

Accommodation options 61

Chapter 1
Introduction

Nestled in the heart of the French Alps, Annecy is a picturesque town that captivates visitors with its stunning natural beauty and rich historical charm. Often referred to as the "Venice of the Alps," Annecy is renowned for its enchanting canals, crystal-clear lake, and charming medieval streets that evoke a sense of timeless elegance.

As you wander through Annecy, you'll be greeted by a vibrant tapestry of experiences. The town's centerpiece is the breathtaking Lake Annecy, renowned for its emerald waters and stunning alpine backdrop. Whether you choose to take a leisurely boat ride, stroll along the lakeside promenades, or simply bask in the serene ambiance, the lake offers a perfect escape into nature.

The old town, with its narrow cobblestone streets and colorful facades, invites you to step back in time. Here, you'll find the Palais de l'Isle, a historic prison turned museum that stands proudly in the center of the Thiou River, and the Château d'Annecy, a majestic castle that overlooks the town and offers panoramic views of the surrounding mountains.

Annecy's rich cultural heritage is celebrated through its vibrant festivals, lively markets, and charming local shops. The town is home to a thriving culinary scene, with delightful restaurants and cafés serving up regional specialties, including the famous Savoyard cheeses and fresh fish from the lake.

This guide is your key to uncovering all that Annecy has to offer. From its top attractions and curated itineraries to hidden treasures and practical tips, you'll find everything you need to make the most of your visit. Dive into the cultural richness, natural beauty, and unique experiences that make Annecy a truly unforgettable destination.

Welcome to Annecy, where every corner holds a story, and every moment offers a chance to create lasting memories.

Geography and overview of Annecy

Annecy: A Jewel in the French Alps

Annecy, often hailed as the "Venice of the Alps," is a charming town located in the Haute-Savoie department of the Auvergne-Rhône-Alpes region in southeastern France. Nestled at the edge of Lake Annecy, the town is surrounded by the majestic peaks of the French Alps, offering a spectacular blend of natural beauty and historical allure.

Geographical Setting

Annecy sits at an altitude of approximately 447 meters (1,467 feet) above sea level. The town is strategically positioned at the foot of the Semnoz mountain range, which forms a stunning backdrop to the picturesque lake. Lake Annecy, with its pristine turquoise waters, is one of the cleanest lakes in Europe, fed by the natural springs of the surrounding mountains. The lake stretches about 14 kilometers (9 miles) in length and 3

- **The Old Town (Vieille Ville):** This historic center is known for its well-preserved medieval architecture, including the Palais de l'Isle, and its charming canals.
- **The Lake Area:** The promenade along Lake Annecy is a focal point for recreational activities and offers stunning views of the lake and mountains.
- **The New Town:** This area features more modern amenities and shopping options, while still maintaining a connection to the town's historical roots.

Connectivity

Annecy is well-connected by road and rail, making it accessible from major cities in France and neighboring countries. The town is approximately 40 kilometers (25 miles) from Geneva, Switzerland, and about 130 kilometers (81 miles) from Lyon, France. The nearby Annecy Haute-Savoie-Mont Blanc Airport provides additional connectivity for travelers arriving by air.

Annecy's unique geographical setting, with its picturesque lake and alpine surroundings, combined with its rich historical and cultural heritage, makes it a captivating destination for visitors. Whether you are drawn to its natural beauty, historical sites, or outdoor activities, Annecy offers a diverse range of experiences that reflect its status as one of France's most enchanting towns.

A brief history of Annecy

Ancient Origins

Annecy's history stretches back to Roman times, though its earliest recorded history begins in the medieval period. The area around Annecy was originally settled by the Celts and later became part of the Roman Empire. Its strategic location along the Thiou River, connecting Lake Annecy to the Rhône River, made it a significant site for trade and transportation.

Medieval Period

In the early medieval period, Annecy was part of the County of Geneva, a significant regional power. The town's importance grew as it became a center of trade and commerce. In the 12th century, the Counts of Geneva built the Château d'Annecy, a fortress that would become a prominent symbol of the town's authority and protection.

Rise of the House of Savoy

During the late medieval period, Annecy came under the control of the House of Savoy, a powerful dynasty that ruled over a vast territory in the Alps. The House of Savoy significantly influenced the town's development, and Annecy became an important administrative and cultural center within their domain. The arrival of the House of Savoy led to a period of prosperity and growth, as they invested in the town's infrastructure and cultural life.

Renaissance and Reformation

The Renaissance brought cultural and architectural developments to Annecy. The town's churches and public buildings from this period reflect the architectural styles of the time. In the 16th century, the Protestant Reformation had a significant impact on the region, leading to religious conflicts and changes in the town's dynamics. Despite these challenges, Annecy remained an important center of trade and culture.

Modern Era

In the 19th century, Annecy underwent significant modernization. The development of transportation infrastructure, including railways, enhanced the town's connectivity and economic growth. The late 19th and early 20th centuries saw the rise of tourism, with visitors drawn to Annecy's picturesque setting and historic charm.

20th Century to Present

During World War II, Annecy was relatively untouched compared to many other European cities, preserving its historical heritage. In the post-war period, the town continued to develop as a tourist destination, attracting visitors with its scenic beauty and historical sites. Today, Annecy is known for its well-preserved medieval architecture, vibrant cultural life, and stunning natural surroundings. It remains a popular destination for travelers seeking a blend of history, culture, and outdoor adventure.

Annecy's rich history reflects its evolution from a medieval trading hub to a charming tourist destination.

Its historical landmarks, such as the Château d'Annecy and the Palais de l'Isle, serve as enduring symbols of the town's storied past. With its blend of historical significance and natural beauty, Annecy continues to captivate visitors from around the world.

Why Annecy should be your next adventure destination

Annecy, often dubbed the "Venice of the Alps," is a destination that promises to captivate every traveler with its breathtaking landscapes and enchanting charm. Nestled between the turquoise waters of Lake Annecy and the majestic peaks of the French Alps, this picturesque town offers a perfect blend of natural beauty and historical allure. Here's why Annecy should be at the top of your adventure list:

1. Majestic Natural Landscapes

Annecy is a haven for outdoor enthusiasts. The pristine Lake Annecy, surrounded by lush forests and towering mountains, provides endless opportunities for adventure. Whether you're into kayaking, sailing, or paddleboarding on the lake, or prefer hiking and cycling along scenic trails with panoramic views, Annecy's natural beauty offers something for everyone. In winter, the nearby ski resorts transform the region into a snowy wonderland, perfect for skiing, snowboarding, and snowshoeing.

2. Rich Historical and Cultural Heritage

Step back in time as you explore Annecy's well-preserved medieval architecture. The Château d'Annecy, with its imposing structure and panoramic views, offers a glimpse into the town's storied past. Wander through the cobbled streets of the Old Town, where the Palais de l'Isle stands as a symbol of the town's historical significance. Annecy's vibrant cultural scene, highlighted by its festivals, local markets, and charming boutiques, provides a deeper understanding of the town's rich heritage.

3. Culinary Delights

Annecy's culinary scene is a treat for the senses. The town's restaurants and cafés serve up delectable Savoyard cuisine, featuring regional specialties such as fondue, raclette, and fresh fish from the lake. Enjoy a meal with a view at one of the lakeside eateries or savor gourmet dishes in the historic heart of the town. The local markets offer a bounty of fresh produce, cheeses, and artisanal goods, perfect for sampling and bringing home a taste of Annecy.

4. Vibrant Festivals and Events

Annecy hosts a range of festivals and events throughout the year, each celebrating its unique cultural heritage. The Annecy International Animated Film Festival attracts global attention with its showcase of innovative animations. The town's lively Christmas markets and summer music festivals provide a festive atmosphere and offer opportunities to immerse yourself in local traditions and celebrations.

5. Relaxation and Wellness

For those seeking relaxation, Annecy offers a tranquil escape with its serene lakefront promenades and lush green spaces. Take a leisurely stroll along the lake, enjoy a picnic in the park, or unwind at a lakeside café. The town's spa and wellness centers provide a perfect retreat for rejuvenation after a day of exploration and adventure.

6. Accessibility and Convenience

Annecy's convenient location, just a short distance from Geneva and Lyon, makes it easily accessible for travelers from across Europe. The town's well-connected transportation network ensures a smooth and enjoyable visit, allowing you to focus on making the most of your adventure.

Annecy's combination of stunning natural landscapes, rich cultural heritage, and diverse recreational opportunities makes it an ideal destination for any traveler seeking adventure and discovery. Whether you're an outdoor enthusiast, a history buff, a foodie, or simply in search of relaxation, Annecy offers an array of experiences that promise to make your trip unforgettable. Embrace the charm and beauty of Annecy—your next great adventure awaits!

Top Destinations and Attractions in Annecy

1. Château d'Annecy

Description: The Château d'Annecy is a grand medieval fortress overlooking the town and Lake Annecy. This imposing structure, originally built in the 12th century, now houses the Musée-Château, featuring exhibits on regional history, art, and archaeology. The castle offers stunning panoramic views of the lake and surrounding Alps.

Location: Place du Château, 74000 Annecy, France

How to Get There:

- **From Annecy Train Station:** Exit the station and walk south towards Rue de la Gare. Follow signs to the Old Town, where the castle is prominently located. The walk takes approximately 10 minutes.
- **By Car:** Drive to Place du Château. Parking is limited, so consider using public transport or parking further away and walking to the castle.
- **By Bike:** Rent a bike and follow the scenic cycle paths towards the Old Town. The ride is enjoyable and allows you to explore Annecy's charming streets en route.

2. Palais de l'Isle

Description: The Palais de l'Isle is a historic building set on a small island in the Thiou River. Originally a medieval prison, it now functions as a museum that showcases Annecy's history and architecture. The building's distinctive triangular shape and picturesque setting make it one of the town's most photographed landmarks.

Location: 3 Passage de l'Isle, 74000 Annecy, France

How to Get There:

- **From Annecy Train Station:** Walk east towards the Old Town, crossing the Thiou River. The Palais de l'Isle is located on a small island, a short 15-minute walk from the station.
- **By Car:** Parking is limited in the Old Town. Use public parking areas such as Parking Préfecture or Parking Notre-Dame and walk to the Palais.
- **By Bike:** Cycle from the city center and cross the bridges leading to the Palais. Bike parking is available nearby.

3. Lake Annecy

Description: Lake Annecy, known for its clear blue waters and stunning alpine scenery, is a major attraction. Visitors can enjoy a variety of activities such as kayaking, paddleboarding, and swimming. The lake's promenade and green spaces are perfect for leisurely walks, picnics, or simply enjoying the serene views.

Location: Lake Annecy, 74000 Annecy, France

How to Get There:

- **From Annecy Train Station:** Walk south from the station towards the lake. The lakefront is a short and scenic walk away.
- **By Car:** Park at one of the nearby parking lots, such as Parking du Paquier or Parking des Marquisats. From there, it's a short walk to the lake's edge.
- **By Bike:** Use the dedicated bike paths around the lake. Renting a bike allows for easy exploration of the lake's perimeter and its picturesque spots.

4. Jardins de l'Europe

Description: The Jardins de l'Europe are beautifully landscaped gardens situated by Lake Annecy. Featuring walking paths, fountains, and well-maintained greenery, these gardens offer a peaceful retreat with stunning views of the lake and mountains. It's an ideal spot for relaxation and enjoying the natural beauty of Annecy.

Location: Boulevard Taine, 74000 Annecy, France

How to Get There:

- **From Annecy Train Station:** Walk south along Boulevard du Paquier to reach the gardens. It's about a 10-minute walk from the station.
- **By Car:** Park at Parking des Marquisats, which is close to the gardens. A short walk will take you to the entrance.
- **By Bike:** Cycle along the lake's edge to reach the Jardins de l'Europe. There are bike racks available near the gardens.

5. Pont des Amours

Description: The Pont des Amours, or "Lovers' Bridge," is a charming pedestrian bridge over the Canal du Vassé. It offers picturesque views of Lake Annecy and is a popular spot for romantic photos and attaching love locks. The bridge's scenic setting makes it a favorite among visitors and couples.

Location: Quai Napoléon III, 74000 Annecy, France

How to Get There:

- **From Annecy Train Station:** Walk towards the lake and follow Quai Napoléon III. The bridge is near the Jardins de l'Europe, making it easily accessible on foot.

- **By Car:** Park at Parking du Paquier or Parking des Marquisats. Both are a short walk from the bridge.

- **By Bike:** Cycle along the lake's edge to reach the Pont des Amours, enjoying the scenic route and convenient bike racks nearby.

6. Musée-Château d'Annecy

Description: The Musée-Château d'Annecy, housed within the Château d'Annecy, offers insights into the region's history and culture. Its exhibits include medieval artifacts, religious art, and historical documents. The museum provides a comprehensive view of Annecy's past, set against the backdrop of the castle's stunning architecture.

Location: Place du Château, 74000 Annecy, France

How to Get There:

- **From Annecy Train Station:** Follow the same route as for Château d'Annecy. The museum is located within the castle, so the directions are the same.
- **By Car:** Park at Place du Château or use nearby public parking. A walk from the parking areas will take you to the museum entrance.
- **By Bike:** Ride through the Old Town to the Château and museum. Bike racks are available for secure parking.

7. Mont Veyrier

Description: Mont Veyrier is a popular hiking destination offering spectacular views of Lake Annecy and the surrounding Alps. The hike to the summit provides a moderate challenge and rewards visitors with panoramic vistas of the lake and the surrounding natural landscape.

Location: Mont Veyrier, 74000 Annecy, France

How to Get There:

- **From Annecy Train Station:** Take a local bus or drive to the base of Mont Veyrier. Trailheads are accessible from the nearby village of Menthon-Saint-Bernard.
- **By Car:** Drive to the trailheads located around Mont Veyrier. Parking is available at the base of the trails.
- **By Public Transport:** Use local buses that head towards nearby villages, then follow signs or maps to the hiking trails.

8. Quartier de la République

Description: The Quartier de la République is a vibrant neighborhood known for its bustling shopping streets, cafés, and diverse dining options. It provides a contrast to the historical charm of the Old Town, offering a taste of modern Annecy with its lively atmosphere and contemporary amenities.

Location: Quartier de la République, 74000 Annecy, France

How to Get There:

- **From Annecy Train Station:** Walk west towards the Quartier de la République. It's about a 10-15 minute walk from the station.
- **By Car:** There is parking available in the area, including public lots and street parking. Be mindful of parking regulations.
- **By Bike:** Cycle from the train station or city center to the Quartier de la République, enjoying the ride through Annecy's streets.

Annecy's top attractions are well-connected and easily accessible, whether you prefer walking, biking, driving, or using public transport.

Chapter 2
Planning Your Trip

Annecy, with its enchanting lakeside setting and picturesque medieval streets, is a destination that promises a memorable experience. Proper planning will ensure you make the most of your visit to this charming town. Here's a comprehensive guide to help you prepare for your trip:

When to Visit

Spring (April to June): Enjoy mild weather, blooming flowers, and fewer crowds. It's ideal for outdoor activities and exploring Annecy's natural beauty.

Summer (July to August): The peak tourist season with warm temperatures and a bustling atmosphere.

Perfect for lake activities and festivals but expect higher prices and crowded attractions.

Fall (September to November): Experience cooler temperatures and beautiful autumn colors. The town is less crowded, offering a more relaxed visit.

Winter (December to February): A quieter time with potential snow and festive holiday decorations. Ideal for a cozy, serene visit.

Getting There

Annecy, nestled in the French Alps, is accessible by various transportation options. Here's how you can reach this picturesque town from different points of origin:

1. By Air

- **Geneva Airport (GVA), Switzerland:** The nearest major airport to Annecy is Geneva Airport, located approximately 45 kilometers (28 miles) from the town. It is well-connected with international flights from major cities around the world.

    How to Get There from Geneva Airport:

    - **By Train:** Take a train from Geneva Airport to Annecy. The journey involves a transfer at Geneva's main train station. Trains run regularly and the total travel time is around 1.5 hours.

- o   **By Bus:** Several shuttle services operate between Geneva Airport and Annecy. The journey typically takes around 1 hour.
- o   **By Car:** Renting a car is a convenient option. Drive east on the A41 motorway, which connects directly to Annecy. The drive takes about 45 minutes.

- **Lyon-Saint Exupéry Airport (LYS):** Located about 150 kilometers (93 miles) from Annecy, Lyon-Saint Exupéry Airport is another option.

How to Get There from Lyon-Saint Exupéry Airport:

- o   **By Train:** Take a train from Lyon-Part-Dieu Station to Annecy, with a transfer at

Geneva or a direct route. The trip takes approximately 2 to 2.5 hours.

- **By Car:** Drive on the A43 and A41 motorways. The journey takes around 2 hours and offers scenic views along the way.

2. By Train

- **From Paris:** Take a high-speed TGV train from Paris Gare du Lyon to Annecy. The journey takes approximately 3 hours and provides a comfortable and scenic route through the French countryside.
- **From Lyon:** Direct TER trains run from Lyon-Part-Dieu Station to Annecy. The travel time is

about 2 hours, making it a convenient option for travelers coming from Lyon.

- **From Geneva:** The train journey from Geneva to Annecy involves a transfer at Geneva's main train station. Total travel time is around 1.5 hours.

3. By Car

- **From Geneva:** Drive east on the A41 motorway, which connects Geneva directly to Annecy. The drive is straightforward and takes about 45 minutes. Be mindful of traffic and parking regulations in Annecy.
- **From Lyon:** Head north on the A43 and then onto the A41 motorway. The drive takes approximately 2 hours, and you'll enjoy scenic views of the Alps along the way.

- **From Paris:** Take the A6 motorway from Paris towards Lyon, then switch to the A40 and A41 motorways. The drive takes around 5 to 6 hours, depending on traffic.

4. **By Bus**

- **Intercity Buses:** Several bus companies operate services to Annecy from major French cities, including Paris, Lyon, and Geneva. The journey time varies but typically ranges from 2 to 5 hours, depending on the departure city.

5. **By Bike**

- **Cycling:** For the adventurous, Annecy is accessible by bike from surrounding areas. The town is well-connected by scenic cycling routes, and you can enjoy the stunning landscapes of the French Alps along the way.

6. Local Transportation

- **Public Transport in Annecy:** Once you arrive in Annecy, the town is well-served by buses and boats. The local transport system makes it easy to explore the town and its surroundings.
- **Car Rentals:** If you prefer to explore the area around Annecy, consider renting a car. Several rental agencies operate in town, and having a car provides flexibility to visit nearby attractions.

Whether you're arriving by air, train, car, or bus, reaching Annecy is straightforward and offers various options to suit your travel preferences. Plan your route in advance to ensure a smooth journey and enjoy the beauty and charm of this delightful French town.

Arrange Transportation (Getting around)

Public Transport: Annecy has an efficient public transport system, including buses and boats. The bus network covers the town and surrounding areas, while boat services offer scenic rides on Lake Annecy.

Walking: Many of Annecy's attractions are within walking distance, especially in the Old Town. Strolling through the streets is a great way to explore and soak in the town's ambiance.

Cycling: Rent a bike to navigate the town and lake paths. Annecy is bike-friendly, with dedicated lanes and scenic routes around the lake.

Car: While driving can be convenient, parking in the Old Town can be challenging. Utilize public parking areas and explore on foot or by bike once you're parked.

Prepare for Activities

Annecy offers a wealth of activities, from outdoor adventures to cultural explorations. To make the most of your time, here's how to prepare for the various experiences awaiting you:

1. **Outdoor Adventures**

- **Hiking and Biking:**
    - **Gear:** Wear comfortable hiking boots or trail shoes, and bring moisture-wicking clothing. For biking, ensure your bike is in

good condition and equipped with appropriate gear.

- **Maps and Trails:** Obtain maps of local trails and biking routes from the Annecy Tourist Office or online resources. Popular trails include the Semnoz and the Doussard Circuit.
- **Weather:** Check the weather forecast before heading out. Weather can change quickly in the Alps, so pack rain gear and dress in layers.

- **Lake Activities:**
  - **Swimming and Boating:** Pack swimwear, sunscreen, and a hat. Rental options for boats, paddleboards, and kayaks are available around Lake Annecy.

- **Fishing:** If you plan to fish, ensure you have a valid fishing license. Check local regulations and bring the necessary equipment.

- **Winter Sports:**
    - **Skiing and Snowboarding:** Bring appropriate winter gear, including ski pants, jackets, gloves, and goggles. Consider renting equipment from local shops if you're not traveling with your own.
    - **Snowshoeing:** Snowshoes can be rented locally. Wear thermal layers, and check for trail conditions and avalanche warnings.

With careful preparation, you can fully enjoy the diverse activities Annecy has to offer. Whether you're hiking in the mountains, exploring historic sites, or relaxing by the lake, being well-prepared will enhance your experience and ensure a smooth and enjoyable trip.

Pack Appropriately

Annecy's diverse activities and changing weather conditions make thoughtful packing essential for a comfortable and enjoyable visit. Here's a comprehensive packing guide to ensure you're well-prepared for your adventure:

1. **Clothing Essentials**

- **Layering Pieces:** Annecy's weather can vary, so packing layers is key. Bring lightweight base layers, a mid-layer for insulation, and a waterproof outer layer.

- **Base Layers:** Moisture-wicking tops and thermal underwear are essential, especially if you're visiting in cooler months or engaging in outdoor activities.
- **Mid-Layers:** Fleece or lightweight sweaters for warmth.
- **Outer Layers:** A waterproof and windproof jacket for rain or snow. A durable raincoat or shell jacket is ideal for outdoor exploration.

- **Casual Wear:** Comfortable clothes for sightseeing, dining, and casual activities. Include:

- **T-Shirts and Long-Sleeve Shirts:** For layering and versatile wear.
- **Jeans or Comfortable Pants:** Suitable for walking and casual outings.
- **Shorts and Dresses:** For warmer weather or if you're visiting in the summer.
- **Formal or Special Occasion Outfits:** If you plan to dine at upscale restaurants or attend special events, pack a smart outfit.
- **Sleepwear:** Comfortable pajamas or sleepwear suited to the season.

2. Footwear

- **Walking Shoes:** Comfortable and supportive shoes for exploring Annecy's streets, attractions, and shopping areas. Opt for shoes with good grip for slippery or uneven surfaces.

- **Outdoor Shoes:** If you're hiking or biking, bring sturdy hiking boots or trail shoes. Ensure they are broken in to prevent blisters.
- **Swimwear:** If you plan to swim or enjoy water activities on Lake Annecy, pack a swimsuit.

3. **Accessories**

- **Sun Protection:** Sunglasses with UV protection, sunscreen with a high SPF, and a wide-brimmed hat to protect against sun exposure.
- **Cold Weather Gear:** If visiting in winter or cooler months, bring gloves, a warm hat, and a scarf.

- **Reusable Water Bottle:** Stay hydrated during your explorations and activities.
- **Umbrella:** A compact, travel-sized umbrella can be useful for unexpected rain.

4. Toiletries and Personal Items

- **Travel Toiletry Kit:** Include essentials such as toothpaste, toothbrush, shampoo, conditioner, soap, and any other personal hygiene products.
- **Medication:** Pack any prescription medications, over-the-counter remedies, and a basic first-aid kit.
- **Personal Items:** Bring any special personal care items you might need, such as contact lenses or feminine hygiene products.

5. Electronics

- **Camera:** A camera or smartphone with a good camera to capture your memories. Don't forget extra batteries or a charger.
- **Phone and Charger:** Ensure your phone is charged and bring a compatible charger.
- **Portable Power Bank:** Handy for charging your devices on the go.
- **Travel Adapter:** If traveling from outside Europe, bring a universal travel adapter to charge your electronic devices.

6. Travel Documents and Essentials

- **Passport and ID:** Ensure your passport is valid for the duration of your stay and carry a form of identification.

- **Travel Insurance:** Bring proof of your travel insurance coverage.

- **Tickets and Reservations:** Print or have digital copies of your flight, train tickets, hotel reservations, and any activity bookings.

- **Local Currency:** Bring some Euros for smaller purchases. Credit and debit cards are widely accepted, but having cash on hand can be helpful.

7. Miscellaneous Items

- **Reusable Shopping Bag:** Useful for groceries or shopping, and environmentally friendly.

- **Small Backpack or Daypack:** Ideal for carrying essentials during day trips and explorations.

By packing appropriately, you'll be well-prepared to enjoy all that Annecy has to offer, from its outdoor adventures to its charming streets. Adjust your packing list based on the season, your planned activities, and personal preferences to ensure a smooth and enjoyable trip.

Final Preparations

As your trip to Annecy approaches, taking care of a few final details will help ensure a smooth and enjoyable experience. Here's a checklist to help you with the final preparations:

1. Confirm Travel Arrangements

- **Flight/Train/Bus Tickets:** Double-check your tickets and reservations. Ensure you have all necessary confirmations and booking references.

- **Accommodation:** Confirm your accommodation details and check-in times. Contact your hotel or rental to confirm any special requests or needs.

- **Transportation:** If you're renting a car, confirm your reservation and ensure you understand the pick-up and drop-off locations.

2. Finalize Packing

- **Packing List:** Review your packing list to ensure you've packed all essentials. Check for any last-minute additions, such as chargers or travel documents.

- **Luggage:** Ensure your luggage is packed securely and is within weight limits. Consider using luggage locks for added security.

3. Health and Safety

- **Travel Insurance:** Confirm your travel insurance details and keep a copy of your policy with you.

- **Vaccinations and Health Precautions:** If necessary, ensure you've received any required vaccinations and are aware of health precautions.

- **Medication:** Pack any medications and medical supplies you may need. Keep a list of any allergies or medical conditions in case of emergencies.

4. Financial Preparations

- **Currency:** Ensure you have enough local currency or a plan to withdraw money upon arrival. Notify your bank of your travel plans to avoid any issues with your credit or debit cards.

- **Emergency Contacts:** Keep a list of emergency contacts, including your bank's contact information, in case you need to report lost or stolen cards.

5. Communication and Connectivity

- **Phone Settings:** Check that your phone plan covers international calls and data or consider purchasing a local SIM card if needed.

- **Contact Information:** Update friends and family with your travel itinerary and contact information in case they need to reach you.

6. Home Preparations

- **Security:** Secure your home before you leave. Arrange for mail collection, and consider setting up timers for lights if you're away for an extended period.
- **Pets and Plants:** Arrange for pet care or plant watering if necessary. Ensure someone will be available to take care of them while you're away.

7. Documents and Important Items

- **Travel Documents:** Make copies of important documents such as your passport, visa (if applicable), travel insurance, and reservation confirmations. Keep them in a separate location from the originals.

- **Emergency Information:** Have a list of local emergency contacts in Annecy, including the nearest hospital, police station, and embassy or consulate information if traveling internationally.

8. Local Research and Planning

- **Itinerary:** Review your planned itinerary and ensure you have all necessary information for tours, activities, and attractions.
- **Local Customs:** Refresh your knowledge of local customs and etiquette to ensure a respectful and enjoyable experience.

- **Weather Check:** Check the weather forecast for Annecy to make any final adjustments to your packing.

9. Relax and Enjoy

- **Rest:** Ensure you get a good night's sleep before your trip to start your journey well-rested.
- **Mindfulness:** Take a moment to relax and mentally prepare for your trip. Being organized and prepared will help you fully enjoy your time in Annecy.

By taking these final preparatory steps, you'll be well-equipped to make the most of your visit to Annecy.

Chapter 3

Accommodation options

Hotels and guesthouses

Annecy offers a range of accommodation options, from luxurious hotels to charming guesthouses, catering to different tastes and budgets. Here's a guide to some of the best hotels and guesthouses in Annecy:

1. Luxury Hotels

- **Les Tresoms Lake and Spa Resort**
    - **Description:** A five-star hotel offering stunning views of Lake Annecy and the surrounding mountains. Features include a spa, gourmet restaurant, and elegant rooms with balconies.

- Location: 15 Boulevard de la Corniche, 74000 Annecy
- Website: Les Tresoms.com

- **L'Impérial Palace**
  - Description: An iconic luxury hotel set in a historic building with refined decor. The hotel boasts a casino, a spa, and panoramic views of the lake.
  - Location: 3 Avenue d'Albigny, 74000 Annecy
  - Website: L'Impérial Palace.com

- **Hotel Le Pre Carre**
  - Description: A chic boutique hotel featuring modern amenities, stylish rooms, and a central location close to Annecy's attractions.
  - Location: 8 Rue Francois de Menthon, 74000 Annecy
  - Website: Hotel Le Pre Carre.com

2. Mid-Range Hotels

- **Hotel Splendid**
    - **Description:** A comfortable three-star hotel with a friendly atmosphere, located a short walk from Lake Annecy. Offers modern rooms and a bar.
    - **Location:** 17 Rue Jean-Jacques Rousseau, 74000 Annecy
    - **Website:** [Hotel Splendid](#).com
- **Hotel du Palais de l'Isle**
    - **Description:** A charming hotel housed in a historic building with unique character. Located in the heart of the old town, it provides easy access to Annecy's main attractions.
    - **Location:** 13 Rue Perrière, 74000 Annecy
    - **Website:** [Hotel du Palais de l'Isle](#).com

- **Best Western Hotel International**
    - **Description:** A modern hotel offering comfortable accommodations and amenities like a fitness center and business services. Centrally located for easy access to the city.
    - **Location:** 19 Avenue du Parmelan, 74000 Annecy
    - **Website:**BestWesternHotelInternational.com

3. Budget-Friendly Hotels and Guesthouses

- **Ibis Annecy**
    - **Description:** A well-known budget hotel chain offering clean, simple rooms and basic amenities. Located near the city center with easy access to local attractions.
    - **Location:** 2 Place Marie Curie, 74000 Annecy

- o   **Website:** Ibis Annecy.com

- **Hotel de Savoie**

    - o   **Description:** A cozy hotel offering comfortable rooms and a central location at a reasonable price. Ideal for travelers looking for a simple and affordable stay.

    - o   **Location:** 1 Place St François de Sales, 74000 Annecy

    - o   **Website:** Hotel de Savoie.com

- **Auberge du Lyonnais**

    - o   **Description:** A charming guesthouse with a traditional ambiance, offering affordable rates and a convenient location near Annecy's old town.

    - o   **Location:** 20 Rue Jean-Jacques Rousseau, 74000 Annecy

    - o   **Website:** Auberge du Lyonnais.com

4. Unique and Boutique Accommodations

- **La Maison de Famille**
    - **Description:** A boutique guesthouse with a homely feel, offering personalized service and cozy, well-decorated rooms. Located in a tranquil area near the lake.
    - **Location:** 7 Rue du Général de Gaulle, 74000 Annecy
    - **Website:** [La Maison de Famille](#).com
- **Château des Avenières**
    - **Description:** Set in a grand château, this guesthouse offers a unique experience with elegant rooms and beautiful grounds. Perfect for a romantic getaway or special occasion.
    - **Location:** 1070 Route de la Chambière, 74800 La Balme-de-Sillingy (close to Annecy)
    - **Website:** [Château des Avenières](#).com

5. Booking Tips

- **Advance Booking:** Annecy is a popular destination, especially during peak tourist seasons. Booking your accommodation well in advance is recommended.
- **Reviews and Ratings:** Check online reviews and ratings to ensure your chosen accommodation meets your expectations and preferences.
- **Location:** Consider the location of your accommodation in relation to the attractions you plan to visit and the convenience of transportation options.

Annecy's accommodation options cater to a wide range of preferences and budgets. Whether you're looking for luxury, comfort, or affordability, you'll find a suitable place to stay in this picturesque city. Book early to secure the best rates and ensure a pleasant stay during

your visit to Annecy.

Chapter 4

Exploring Annecy

Off the beaten track: discover lesser-known hiking trails and attractions

While Annecy is famous for its stunning lake and picturesque old town, there are many hidden gems waiting to be discovered away from the crowds.

1. Le Roc des Boeufs

- **Description:** Le Roc des Boeufs is a lesser-known peak that offers a tranquil hiking experience with stunning views over the Bauges and Aravis mountain ranges. The trail is ideal for those seeking a peaceful escape.
- **Trail Details:** The hike starts from the village of La Clusaz and involves a moderate ascent through alpine meadows and forests. The summit provides panoramic views and a chance to enjoy the quiet beauty of the area.
- **How to Get There:** Drive to La Clusaz and park near the trailhead. Look for signs indicating the route to Le Roc des Boeufs.

2. Cascade du Pissieu

- **Description:** Hidden in the forests near the village of Saint-Jorioz, the Cascade du Pissieu is a picturesque waterfall that's often overlooked by tourists. It's a great spot for a peaceful nature walk and a refreshing break.

- **Trail Details:** The trail to the waterfall is relatively easy and suitable for families. It takes you through lush woodland, with the waterfall as a rewarding destination.

- **How to Get There:** Drive to Saint-Jorioz and follow signs to the Cascade du Pissieu. There are designated parking areas and trail markers to guide you.

3. Plateau des Glières

- **Description:** The Plateau des Glières is a high-altitude plateau known for its historical significance and natural beauty. It's a fantastic spot for hiking and exploring less-trodden paths amidst stunning landscapes.

- **Trail Details:** The area offers various hiking routes, including trails that pass through historical sites and scenic viewpoints. The terrain ranges from gentle slopes to more challenging paths.

- **How to Get There:** Drive to the Plateau des Glières, which is accessible via a mountain road. Parking is available at the plateau's main entrance, where you can find trail information and maps.

4. Le Col de la Forclaz

- **Description:** Le Col de la Forclaz is a mountain pass with panoramic views of Lake Annecy and the surrounding peaks. It's a quieter alternative to more popular viewpoints and offers excellent hiking opportunities.
- **Trail Details:** The hike to the col is moderate, with well-marked trails and beautiful scenery.

The pass itself provides stunning vistas and a chance to enjoy the peaceful surroundings.

- **How to Get There:** Drive to the Col de la Forclaz via a scenic mountain road. There are parking areas near the pass, and trails are easily accessible from there.

5. La Grotte de la Baume

- **Description:** The Grotte de la Baume is a lesser-known cave system near Annecy, offering a fascinating underground exploration experience. The cave is less frequented, providing a more intimate adventure.
- **Trail Details:** The cave features guided tours that showcase its natural formations and geological history. It's a great option for those interested in exploring Annecy's natural wonders.
- **How to Get There:** Drive to the village of Seynod and follow signs to the Grotte de la Baume. Guided tours are available, so check in advance for scheduling and availability.

Chapter 5

Immerse yourself in the local culture

Cultural experiences beyond the surface: authentic encounters and traditions

Annecy is renowned for its picturesque beauty, but delving deeper into its cultural heritage reveals a rich tapestry of authentic experiences and traditions. Here's a guide to exploring the lesser-known cultural facets of this charming city:

1. Traditional Savoyard Cuisine

- **Description:** Savoyard cuisine is an integral part of Annecy's cultural heritage. Delight in local specialties like raclette, fondue, and tartiflette, which showcase the region's hearty, cheese-centric dishes.

- **Where to Experience:** Visit local bistros and restaurants such as **La Table de Dany** or **Le Clos de la Palud** to enjoy authentic Savoyard meals. These eateries often serve traditional dishes prepared with local ingredients.
- **Tip:** Pair your meal with a local Savoie wine for an authentic culinary experience.

2. **Annecy's Old Town Markets**

- **Description:** The markets in Annecy's Old Town offer a vibrant display of local produce, crafts, and regional specialties. These markets provide a glimpse into the daily life and traditions of the local people.

- **Where to Explore:** Visit the **Marché de la vieille ville** held on Tuesdays, Fridays, and Sundays, where you can find everything from fresh produce to artisanal goods.
- **Tip:** Engage with local vendors to learn about the ingredients and products that define the region's cuisine.

3. The Fête du Lac

- **Description:** The Fête du Lac (Lake Festival) is an annual event celebrating Lake Annecy with a spectacular display of fireworks, music, and performances. It's a vibrant reflection of the city's festive spirit and community involvement.

- **When to Visit:** The festival usually takes place in early August. Plan your visit around this time to witness this grand celebration.
- **Tip:** Arrive early to secure a good spot along the lake for the best views of the fireworks.

4. The Museum of the Resistance and Deportation

- **Description:** This museum offers an in-depth look at the local history of resistance during World War II. It provides valuable insights into the region's wartime experiences and the bravery of those who resisted.
- **Where to Visit:** Located at **14 Rue du 30ème Régiment d'Infanterie**, the museum features exhibits on resistance activities and personal stories from the war.

- **Tip:** Allocate a few hours to fully explore the museum and gain a deeper understanding of the historical context.

5. Craft Workshops and Artisan Studios

- **Description:** Engage in hands-on experiences by participating in workshops that showcase traditional Savoyard crafts. From pottery and weaving to woodwork, these workshops provide a unique opportunity to learn from skilled artisans.
- **Where to Participate:** Look for local studios and workshops such as **Les Ateliers d'Artistes** or **La Maison des Artisans**.
- **Tip:** Check schedules in advance and book your spot early to ensure availability.

6. Local Festivals and Events

- **Description:** Annecy hosts various local festivals throughout the year, including traditional events like the **Festival of the Lake** and **Saint Bernard Fair**, which celebrate local customs and community spirit.
- **When to Attend:** Check the city's event calendar for festival dates and times. These events are excellent for experiencing local traditions and community gatherings.
- **Tip:** Participate in festival activities and interact with locals to fully immerse yourself in the cultural atmosphere.

7. Historical Walking Tours

- **Description:** Join guided walking tours to explore Annecy's rich history and cultural heritage. These tours often include visits to historical sites, old neighborhoods, and significant landmarks.
- **Where to Book:** Tours can be booked through local agencies such as **Annecy Tourisme** or **GetYourGuide**.
- **Tip:** Choose tours led by knowledgeable guides who can provide in-depth commentary and personal anecdotes about the city's history.

8. Visit Local Art Galleries and Exhibitions

- **Description:** Explore Annecy's artistic side by visiting local galleries and exhibitions that showcase regional art and craftsmanship. Discover works by local artists and learn about the artistic influences in the region.

- **Where to Visit:** Galleries such as **Galerie d'Art du Cloître** and **Espace Culturel Louis-Soutter** often feature rotating exhibitions and local art.
- **Tip:** Attend gallery openings or artist talks to gain deeper insights into the local art scene.

9. Attend a Traditional Music Performance

- **Description:** Experience the sounds of traditional Savoyard music by attending performances that feature folk music and local instruments. These performances offer a glimpse into the region's musical heritage.

- **Where to Find Performances:** Check local event listings for performances at venues like **Le Brise Glace** or **Salle des Fêtes**.
- **Tip:** Look for performances that include audience participation for an interactive experience.

10. Explore Local Folklore and Legends

- **Description:** Dive into the folklore and legends of Annecy by exploring stories and myths that have shaped the region's cultural identity. Local legends often provide intriguing insights into the area's historical and cultural landscape.
- **Where to Explore:** Visit local libraries, historical societies, or cultural centers to find books and resources on Annecy's folklore.

- **Tip:** Join local storytelling events or guided tours that focus on folklore for a more immersive experience.

Annecy offers a wealth of cultural experiences beyond its well-known attractions. By engaging with local traditions, exploring lesser-known sites, and participating in authentic cultural activities, you'll gain a deeper appreciation of this charming city and its vibrant heritage. Enjoy your journey into the heart of Annecy's cultural landscape!

Chapter 6

Culinary delights and outdoor adventures

Annecy is not only a visual feast with its picturesque landscapes but also a haven for those who appreciate fine cuisine and outdoor exploration. Here's a guide to enjoying the best of both worlds in this charming city:

Culinary Delights

1. Savoyard Specialties

- **Description:** Annecy is famous for its hearty Savoyard cuisine, which includes dishes such as fondue, raclette, and tartiflette. These traditional meals are perfect for warming up after a day of outdoor activities.

- **Where to Dine:**
    - **La Table de Dany** – Offers an authentic fondue experience with a cozy atmosphere.
    - **Le Clos de la Palud** – Known for its traditional raclette and other Savoyard specialties.
- **Tip:** Pair your meal with a local Savoie wine for a true taste of the region.

2. Gourmet Markets

- **Description:** Explore the vibrant markets in Annecy to discover local produce, cheeses, meats, and pastries. These markets offer a chance to sample and purchase regional delicacies.
- **Where to Visit:**

- o **Marché de la Vieille Ville** – Held on Tuesdays, Fridays, and Sundays, this market features a wide range of local goods.
- o **Marché de Seynod** – Another excellent market with a variety of fresh produce and local treats.
- **Tip:** Look for local specialties such as the delectable blue cheese from the Savoie region.

3. Fine Dining

- **Description:** For a more refined dining experience, Annecy boasts several high-end restaurants that showcase gourmet French cuisine with a contemporary twist.
- **Where to Dine:**

- **L'Auberge du Père Bise** – Renowned for its Michelin-starred dishes and stunning views of the lake.
- **Le Belvédère** – Offers sophisticated French cuisine with a focus on seasonal ingredients.

- **Tip:** Make reservations in advance, especially during peak seasons, to secure a table at these popular spots.

4. Pastry Shops and Cafés

- **Description:** Enjoy the sweet side of Annecy by visiting local pastry shops and cafés. Treat yourself to freshly baked croissants, pastries, and cakes.
- **Where to Visit:**

- - **Pâtisserie J. Chanet** – Famous for its exquisite pastries and cakes.
  - **Café Brunet** – A charming spot for coffee and traditional French sweets.
- **Tip:** Try the local specialty, the "Tarte aux Myrtilles," made with delicious blueberries from the region.

Outdoor Adventures

1. Lake Annecy

- **Description:** Lake Annecy is a stunning natural attraction that offers a range of outdoor activities including swimming, boating, and cycling along its scenic shores.
- **Activities:**

- o **Swimming** – The lake's clear waters are ideal for a refreshing dip.
- o **Boat Rentals** – Rent a pedal boat, rowboat, or electric boat to explore the lake at your own pace.
- o **Cycling** – Follow the dedicated bike paths around the lake for a scenic ride.
- **Tip:** Visit **Plage d'Albigny** for a well-equipped beach area perfect for families.

2. Hiking in the Bauges Mountains

- **Description:** The Bauges Mountains offer a network of trails for all levels of hikers, with routes that provide spectacular views and opportunities to connect with nature.
- **Popular Trails:**

- **Grand Colombier** – A challenging hike with panoramic views of the Alps and Lake Annecy.
- **Sentier des Chamois** – A moderate trail that winds through beautiful alpine landscapes.

- **Tip:** Bring appropriate hiking gear and check trail conditions before setting out.

3. Paragliding

- **Description:** For a truly exhilarating experience, try paragliding over Lake Annecy. Soar high above the lake and take in breathtaking aerial views of the surrounding landscapes.
- **Where to Book:**

- o **Annecy Parapente** – Offers tandem flights with experienced instructors.
- o **Fly Annecy** – Provides paragliding lessons and scenic flights.
- **Tip:** Book in advance and choose a day with clear weather for the best experience.

4. Cycling and Mountain Biking

- **Description:** Annecy is a great destination for cycling enthusiasts, with a variety of routes ranging from leisurely lakeside rides to challenging mountain biking trails.
- **Routes:**
  - o **Lakeside Cycle Path** – A flat, scenic route perfect for a relaxing ride.

- o **La Clusaz Bike Park** – Offers trails for mountain biking with various difficulty levels.
- **Tip:** Rent bikes from local shops such as **Cyclo-Loc** or **Vélocité** for a day of exploration.

5. **Exploring the Semnoz**

- **Description:** The Semnoz is a popular destination for both summer and winter sports. It offers hiking trails, mountain biking routes, and, in the winter, skiing and snowboarding opportunities.
- **Activities:**
  - o **Summer Hiking** – Enjoy well-marked trails with panoramic views.

- ○ **Winter Sports** – Ski or snowboard at the Semnoz Ski Resort.
- **Tip:** Check seasonal conditions and opening times before planning your visit.

6. Water Sports

- **Description:** Engage in various water sports on Lake Annecy, including kayaking, paddleboarding, and windsurfing.
- **Where to Rent Gear:**
    - ○ **Annecy Nautique** – Offers equipment rentals and lessons for water sports.
    - ○ **Paddle & Sail** – Specializes in paddleboarding and kayaking rentals.
- **Tip:** Choose a calm day with favorable weather conditions for the best water sports experience.

Chapter 7

Relaxation and wellness in Annecy

Annecy is not only a hub of picturesque scenery and outdoor adventures but also a sanctuary for relaxation and wellness. The city offers a range of experiences designed to rejuvenate both body and mind. Here's a guide to enjoying the best of relaxation and wellness in Annecy:

1. Spa Experiences

Le Spa des Marquis

- **Description:** This luxurious spa offers a variety of treatments designed to relax and rejuvenate. From soothing massages to revitalizing facials,

Le Spa des Marquis provides a serene environment perfect for unwinding.

- **Location:** 36 Rue du Mont-Blanc, Annecy
- **Tip:** Book treatments in advance to ensure availability and enjoy their signature packages for a complete relaxation experience.

Les Thermes de Marlioz

- **Description:** Located a short drive from Annecy, this thermal spa features natural hot springs and a comprehensive wellness center. Enjoy thermal baths, sauna, and a range of therapeutic treatments.
- **Location:** 9 Avenue des Thermes, Aix-les-Bains
- **Tip:** Combine your visit with a stay at the adjacent hotel for a full wellness retreat.

Hôtel des Alpes Spa

- **Description:** This hotel features an in-house spa offering massages, body scrubs, and other relaxation therapies. The tranquil atmosphere and expert treatments make it a great choice for relaxation.
- **Location:** 4 Boulevard du Président Wilson, Annecy
- **Tip:** Use the spa facilities as part of a stay at the hotel or book a day pass for access.

2. Yoga and Meditation

Annecy Yoga Studio

- **Description:** This local studio offers a variety of yoga classes including Vinyasa, Hatha, and restorative yoga. Perfect for beginners and experienced practitioners alike.

- **Location:** 23 Rue des Frères Lumière, Annecy
- **Tip:** Check the schedule for drop-in classes and workshops. Many studios also offer online sessions.

Zen et Bien-Être

- **Description:** Specializing in meditation and relaxation techniques, this center provides guided meditation sessions and mindfulness workshops to help you de-stress and find inner peace.
- **Location:** 15 Rue des Alpes, Annecy
- **Tip:** Join a group session or book a private meditation class for personalized guidance.

3. Scenic Relaxation

Lakeside Relaxation

- **Description:** The shores of Lake Annecy provide the perfect setting for relaxation. Enjoy a leisurely stroll, relax on the beach, or simply sit by the water and take in the beautiful views.
- **Popular Spots:**
    - **Plage d'Albigny** – A well-maintained beach with amenities.
    - **Plage de l'Imperial** – Offers a quieter spot for peaceful relaxation.
- **Tip:** Bring a picnic and enjoy a tranquil afternoon by the lake.

Parc Charles Bosson

- **Description:** This park offers beautiful green spaces and panoramic views of Lake Annecy. Ideal for a leisurely walk or a relaxing afternoon surrounded by nature.
- **Location:** Avenue de Brogny, Annecy
- **Tip:** Find a comfortable spot under the trees and enjoy some quiet time with a book or simply soak in the natural beauty.

4. Wellness Retreats

Château de Novel

- **Description:** This elegant château offers a comprehensive wellness retreat including spa treatments, yoga classes, and gourmet healthy dining. The setting combines luxury with relaxation in a beautiful natural environment.

- **Location:** 14 Rue du Château, Annecy
- **Tip:** Consider a multi-day retreat to fully immerse yourself in relaxation and wellness activities.

Les Pénates du Lac

- **Description:** Located near Lake Annecy, this retreat offers tailored wellness programs including detox plans, fitness sessions, and personalized treatments designed to rejuvenate and restore balance.
- **Location:** 5 Rue du Vieux Pont, Annecy
- **Tip:** Explore their packages for a customized wellness experience that suits your needs.

5. Outdoor Activities for Relaxation

Guided Nature Walks

- **Description:** Join a guided nature walk to explore the scenic beauty of the surrounding countryside. These walks offer a relaxing way to enjoy the natural landscape and reduce stress.
- **Popular Trails:**
    - **Sentier des Lavandières** – A gentle trail along the lake.
    - **Col de la Forclaz** – Offers panoramic views and peaceful surroundings.
- **Tip:** Choose a guided tour to enhance your experience with local insights and knowledge.

Cycling Around the Lake

- **Description:** A leisurely bike ride around Lake Annecy provides a relaxing way to enjoy the stunning scenery. Many bike rental shops offer bikes suited for a comfortable ride.
- **Route:** The dedicated bike path around the lake is flat and easy, making it accessible for all levels.
- **Tip:** Rent a bike from a local shop and stop at scenic points along the way for breaks and relaxation.

Annecy offers a variety of relaxation and wellness options, from luxurious spa treatments to serene lakeside moments. Whether you're looking to unwind with a massage, find inner peace through yoga, or simply enjoy the natural beauty of the region, Annecy provides the perfect setting for rejuvenation and well-being.

Chapter 8
Practical information

Currency and money matters

Navigating currency and money matters is essential for a smooth and enjoyable visit to Annecy. Here's a guide to help you manage your finances while exploring this beautiful French city.

1. Currency

- **Currency:** The official currency of France is the Euro (€).
- **Current Exchange Rate:** Exchange rates fluctuate, so it's a good idea to check the latest rates before you travel. You can use currency conversion apps or websites for up-to-date information.

2. Currency Exchange

Airport and Train Station Exchanges

- **Description:** Currency exchange services are available at Annecy's train station and nearby Geneva Airport. These locations offer convenience upon arrival.
- **Location:**
    - **Annecy Train Station** – Currency exchange kiosks are typically available.
    - **Geneva Airport** – A larger range of currency exchange services and better rates.
- **Tip:** Exchange a small amount of money at the airport or train station for immediate expenses, then seek better rates in the city.

Banks and Exchange Offices

- **Description:** Banks and dedicated currency exchange offices in Annecy offer competitive rates for exchanging currency.
- **Popular Locations:**
    - **Banque Populaire** – Offers currency exchange services and is centrally located.
    - **Exchange Offices** – Several offices in the city center provide currency exchange.
- **Tip:** Compare rates between different banks and exchange offices for the best deal.

ATMs

- **Description:** ATMs are widely available in Annecy, allowing you to withdraw Euros using your debit or credit card.

- **Locations:** ATMs can be found at major banks, shopping centers, and convenience stores.
- **Tip:** Check with your bank about international withdrawal fees and daily withdrawal limits.

3. Using Credit and Debit Cards

Acceptance

- **Description:** Credit and debit cards are widely accepted in Annecy, including at hotels, restaurants, shops, and attractions.
- **Card Types:** Visa and Mastercard are commonly accepted. American Express may be less widely accepted.
- **Tip:** Inform your bank or card provider about your travel plans to avoid any issues with your cards.

Contactless Payments

- **Description:** Many establishments accept contactless payments, which offer a quick and convenient way to pay using your card or smartphone.
- **Tip:** Ensure your card or smartphone is set up for contactless payments to make transactions easier.

4. Budgeting

Typical Costs

- **Dining:** Expect to spend around €15-€30 for a meal at a mid-range restaurant. A coffee or pastry at a café may cost around €3-€7.
- **Accommodation:** Hotel prices range from €70-€150 per night for mid-range options. Luxury hotels can be significantly more expensive.

- **Transport:** Public transportation such as buses or boats around the lake may cost around €1.50-€5 per ride. Car rentals and taxis will be more expensive.

Tipping

- **Description:** Tipping in France is not compulsory but appreciated. It's common to round up the bill or leave a small amount (5-10%) for good service.
- **Tip:** Check if a service charge is included in your bill before deciding on additional tips.

5. Safety and Security

Avoiding Scams

- **Description:** Be cautious of unofficial currency exchange services and high fees. Use reputable banks and exchange offices for transactions.

- **Tip:** Always count your money carefully and be aware of your surroundings when using ATMs or handling cash.

Keeping Money Safe

- **Description:** Use a money belt or secure wallet to keep your cash and cards safe. Avoid carrying large amounts of cash and use ATMs in well-lit, busy areas.
- **Tip:** Consider using a credit card with fraud protection for additional security.

Managing currency and money matters effectively ensures a smooth and enjoyable experience in Annecy. From exchanging Euros to using credit cards and budgeting wisely, these tips will help you handle your finances with ease while exploring the city.

Safety Tips and Emergency Contact Information

Annecy is generally a safe destination for travelers, but it's always wise to be aware of safety considerations to ensure a smooth and enjoyable visit. Here's a guide to help you stay safe while exploring this picturesque French city.

1. General Safety

Crime Rate

- **Description:** Annecy is known for its low crime rate, making it a safe place for tourists. However, petty crimes such as pickpocketing can occur, especially in crowded areas.

- **Tip:** Remain vigilant in busy areas like markets, public transportation, and tourist hotspots.

Emergency Services

In Annecy, as with the rest of France, several key emergency contact numbers are available to ensure your safety and well-being during your trip:

1. **General Emergency Number (European Emergency Number): 112**
    - This number can be dialed for any emergency across the European Union. It connects you to police, medical services, and fire departments.
2. **Police (Gendarmerie): 17**

- Use this number to contact the local police in case of crime, theft, or other law enforcement-related emergencies.

3. **Fire Brigade (Pompiers): 18**
    - For fire emergencies or accidents requiring immediate assistance, call this number.

4. **Ambulance/Medical Emergency (SAMU): 15**
    - If you or someone with you requires urgent medical attention, dial 15 for an ambulance.

5. **Poison Control Center: +33 (0)1 40 05 48 48**
    - For emergencies related to poisoning, this is the number to call.

6. **Local Hospital in Annecy: Centre Hospitalier Annecy Genevois (CHANGE)**

- **Address:** 1 Avenue de l'Hôpital, 74370 Metz-Tessy, Annecy, France
- **Phone:** +33 4 50 63 63 63

2. *Personal Safety*

Avoiding Pickpockets

- **Description:** Pickpocketing can occur in crowded places and on public transportation.
- **Tip:** Use a money belt or neck pouch to keep valuables secure. Avoid carrying large amounts of cash and be cautious when handling your belongings.

Safe Travel Practices

- **Description:** Stick to well-lit, populated areas, especially at night.

- **Tip:** Use reputable transportation services and avoid accepting offers from strangers.

3. Health and Wellness

Medical Care

- **Description:** France has high-quality healthcare services. If you need medical attention, visit a local pharmacy for minor issues or the hospital for more serious conditions.
- **Tip:** It's advisable to have travel insurance that covers medical expenses.

Pharmacies

- **Description:** Pharmacies are readily available throughout Annecy for prescription medications, over-the-counter remedies, and health advice.

- **Locations:**
  - **Pharmacie du Lac** – 10 Quai de l'Isle, Annecy.
  - **Pharmacie des Alpes** – 4 Rue de la Gare, Annecy.

4. Transportation Safety

Public Transportation

- **Description:** Public transport in Annecy, including buses and boats, is generally safe and reliable.
- **Tip:** Be cautious of your belongings on public transportation and avoid traveling alone late at night if possible.

Taxis and Ride-Sharing

- **Description:** Use official taxis or reputable ride-sharing services like Uber. Avoid hailing taxis from the street; instead, use designated taxi stands or apps.
- **Tip:** Confirm the taxi fare or use an app to ensure fair pricing.

Cycling and Walking

- **Description:** Annecy is bike-friendly with designated cycling paths. Walking is also a safe and enjoyable way to explore the city.
- **Tip:** Follow local traffic rules and be mindful of cyclists and pedestrians.

5. Natural Safety

Weather Considerations

- **Description:** Annecy experiences a range of weather conditions, including occasional heavy rain and winter snow.
- **Tip:** Check weather forecasts before your trip and pack appropriate clothing. Be cautious when walking on icy or wet surfaces.

Outdoor Activities

- **Description:** Activities such as hiking and boating are popular in Annecy. Follow safety guidelines for outdoor adventures.

- **Tip:** Stick to marked trails for hiking and ensure you have the necessary equipment and local knowledge. Always use life jackets when boating.

Annecy is a safe and welcoming destination, with general precautions ensuring a pleasant visit. By staying aware of your surroundings, using reputable services, and preparing for health and weather conditions, you can enjoy all that this beautiful city has to offer with peace of mind.

Chapter 9
Itinerary for Annecy: 5-Day Guide

Annecy, with its stunning lake, charming old town, and scenic surroundings, offers a variety of experiences for a memorable 5-day trip. Here's a detailed itinerary to help you make the most of your visit.

Day 1: Exploring Annecy's Historic Charm

Morning:

- **Old Town (Vieille Ville)**
    - **Description:** Begin your journey in Annecy's picturesque Old Town. Wander through its narrow, winding streets, admire the colorful

buildings, and visit the charming shops and cafes.
- **Highlights:** Explore the Place du Palais de Justice and the Rue Sainte-Claire.

- **Palais de l'Isle**
  - **Description:** This iconic medieval building on the Thiou River is a symbol of Annecy. It once served as a prison and now houses a local history museum.
  - **Location:** Place du Palais de l'Isle, Annecy
  - **Tip:** Check out the museum's exhibits on Annecy's history and architecture.

Afternoon:

- **Annecy Cathedral (Cathédrale Saint-Pierre)**

- Description: Visit this historic cathedral with its beautiful Gothic architecture and serene interior.
- Location: Place Notre-Dame, Annecy

- **Lunch: Le Freti**
  - Description: Enjoy traditional Savoyard cuisine, including fondue and raclette, at this cozy restaurant.
  - Location: 18 Rue de la République, Annecy

Evening:

- **Stroll Along Lake Annecy**
  - Description: Relax with a leisurely walk along the lake's promenade, taking in the serene views and sunset.
  - Location: Lakeside paths near the Palais de l'Isle

- **Dinner: La Table d'Elise**
    - **Description:** Dine at this elegant restaurant offering French cuisine and local specialties.
    - **Location:** 24 Rue du Pont Neuf, Annecy

Day 2: Discovering the Lake and Surroundings

Morning:

- **Boat Tour on Lake Annecy**
    - **Description:** Take a boat tour to enjoy the stunning views of the lake and surrounding mountains.
    - **Location:** Depart from the Annecy Port
    - **Tip:** Choose a guided tour for interesting insights into the lake's history and landmarks.
- **Visit the Château d'Annecy**

- o **Description:** Explore this historic castle, which now houses a museum with exhibits on local history and art.
- o **Location:** Place du Château, Annecy
- o **Tip:** Climb the tower for panoramic views of the city and lake.

Afternoon:

- **Lunch: Brasserie des Alpes**
  - o **Description:** Enjoy a relaxed meal with a range of traditional French dishes.
  - o **Location:** 1 Avenue de Chambéry, Annecy
- **Parc Charles Bosson**
  - o **Description:** Spend the afternoon in this beautiful park, offering expansive green spaces and lake views.
  - o **Location:** Avenue de Brogny, Annecy

Evening:

- **Dinner: La Ciboulette**
    - **Description:** Savor innovative French cuisine at this stylish restaurant.
    - **Location:** 5 Rue de la Poste, Annecy
- **Evening Walk in the Old Town**
    - **Description:** Enjoy the charming ambiance of the Old Town in the evening, with its lit-up streets and peaceful atmosphere.

Day 3: Day Trip to the Surrounding Nature

Morning:

- **Visit to Semnoz**
    - **Description:** Take a day trip to the Semnoz mountain, perfect for hiking and enjoying panoramic views.

- - **Location:** About a 30-minute drive from Annecy
  - **Tip:** Pack appropriate hiking gear and check weather conditions before heading out.

Afternoon:

- **Lunch: Picnic on Semnoz**
  - **Description:** Pack a picnic to enjoy in the scenic mountain environment.
- **Explore the Trails**
  - **Description:** Choose from various hiking trails, ranging from easy walks to more challenging routes.

Evening:

- **Return to Annecy**
  - **Dinner: L'Esquisse**

- **Description:** Indulge in a gourmet dinner featuring local ingredients and creative dishes.
- **Location:** 1 Rue Jean-Jacques Rousseau, Annecy

Day 4: Cultural and Relaxation Experiences

Morning:

- **Annecy Market**
  - **Description:** Visit the local market to experience the vibrant atmosphere and shop for local produce and crafts.
  - **Location:** Place des Halles, Annecy
  - **Tip:** The market is held on Tuesdays, Fridays, and Sundays.
- **Visit to the Palais de l'Isle Museum**

- Description: Explore the museum to learn more about Annecy's history and architecture.
- Location: Place du Palais de l'Isle, Annecy

Afternoon:

- **Lunch: Café Bunna**
    - Description: Enjoy a light lunch at this cozy café offering sandwiches, pastries, and coffee.
    - Location: 16 Rue de la République, Annecy
- **Spa Afternoon: Le Spa des Marquis**
    - Description: Pamper yourself with a relaxing spa treatment at this luxurious spa.
    - Location: 36 Rue du Mont-Blanc, Annecy
    - Tip: Book treatments in advance for a stress-free experience.

Evening:

- **Dinner: La Savoie**
    - **Description:** Experience traditional Savoyard cuisine with a modern twist.
    - **Location:** 7 Rue du Pont Neuf, Annecy
- **Evening Boat Ride**
    - **Description:** Enjoy a peaceful evening boat ride on Lake Annecy, taking in the tranquil surroundings.

Day 5: Outdoor Adventures and Farewell

Morning:

- **Hike to Lake of the Pâquier**
    - **Description:** Take a scenic hike to the Lake of the Pâquier, a picturesque spot ideal for a leisurely walk.

- Location: Near the lake's edge, accessible from Annecy's town center

Afternoon:

- **Lunch: Le Bistrot du Palais**
    - Description: Enjoy a casual lunch featuring local French cuisine.
    - Location: 10 Rue du Palais de Justice, Annecy
- **Relax by the Lake**
    - Description: Spend your final afternoon relaxing by Lake Annecy, perhaps enjoying a paddle boat or simply taking in the views.

Evening:

- **Dinner: Le Coq en Pâte**

- **Description:** Savor your final dinner in Annecy at this charming restaurant known for its creative dishes.
- **Location:** 8 Rue de l'Évêché, Annecy

- **Farewell Walk**
  - **Description:** Take a final stroll through the Old Town, savoring the atmosphere and reflecting on your trip.

This 5-day itinerary provides a mix of historical exploration, natural beauty, cultural experiences, and relaxation, ensuring a well-rounded and memorable visit to Annecy. Enjoy your trip and make the most of the city's charming ambiance and stunning surroundings!

Chapter 10

Summary and Conclusion

Annecy, known as the "Venice of the Alps," is a picturesque city renowned for its stunning lake, charming old town, and surrounding natural beauty. With its rich history, vibrant cultural scene, and outdoor adventures, Annecy offers an array of experiences for travelers. Here's a summary and conclusion based on the comprehensive travel guide provided:

Summary

Introduction Annecy welcomes visitors with its golden splendor and vibrant charm. From the historic streets of the Old Town to the serene beauty of Lake Annecy, the city invites exploration and discovery.

Geography and Overview Nestled in the Auvergne-Rhône-Alpes region of southeastern France, Annecy boasts a stunning lake surrounded by majestic mountains. Its scenic beauty and well-preserved architecture make it a captivating destination.

A Brief History Annecy's history is marked by its role as a medieval stronghold and later as a center of the Protestant Reformation. Its evolution from a fortified town to a charming city is reflected in its preserved landmarks and historical sites.

Why Annecy Should Be Your Next Adventure Destination Annecy combines natural beauty with rich cultural experiences, offering a unique blend of outdoor adventures, historical exploration, and authentic local encounters. It's an ideal destination for those seeking a memorable and diverse travel experience.

Top Destinations and Attractions

1. **Lake Annecy:** A crystal-clear lake perfect for boat tours, swimming, and scenic walks.
2. **Palais de l'Isle:** A historic building and museum offering insights into Annecy's past.
3. **Château d'Annecy:** A castle with panoramic views and historical exhibits.

4. **Old Town (Vieille Ville):** A charming area with colorful buildings, shops, and cafes.
5. **Semnoz Mountain:** A nearby destination for hiking and breathtaking views.

Planning Your Trip Consider the best times to visit, pack appropriately, and make final preparations, including securing accommodation and understanding currency exchange.

Hotels and Guesthouses Annecy offers a range of accommodation options from luxurious hotels to cozy guesthouses, catering to various budgets and preferences.

Off the Beaten Track Discover lesser-known hiking trails and attractions, such as scenic paths around Lake Annecy and hidden gems in the surrounding nature.

Cultural Experiences Beyond the Surface Engage in authentic local traditions and encounters, including traditional Savoyard cuisine, local festivals, and artisan workshops.

Culinary Delights and Outdoor Adventures Savor Annecy's diverse culinary offerings, from local specialties to gourmet dining, and explore outdoor activities like hiking, boating, and relaxing by the lake.

Relaxation and Wellness Enjoy wellness options such as spa treatments and relaxation spots around the lake and parks.

Currency and Money Matters Manage your finances effectively with information on currency exchange, using credit/debit cards, and budgeting for your trip.

Safety Information Annecy is a safe destination with general safety tips, emergency services information, and advice on staying healthy and secure during your visit.

Itinerary for Annecy: 5-Day Guide Experience Annecy's highlights with a structured 5-day itinerary that includes exploring the Old Town, enjoying boat tours, hiking in the surrounding nature, and immersing yourself in local culture and cuisine.

Conclusion

Annecy offers a captivating blend of natural beauty, historical charm, and vibrant culture. Whether you're exploring the historic streets, enjoying the pristine lake, or venturing into the surrounding mountains, the city promises a diverse and enriching experience. This comprehensive guide provides all the essential information to help you plan, explore, and enjoy Annecy to the fullest. Embrace the unique blend of adventure, relaxation, and cultural immersion that Annecy has to offer, and make the most of your visit to this enchanting French gem.

Feel free to adapt any details to better fit your preferences and needs as you prepare for your trip to Annecy!

Printed in Great Britain
by Amazon